Multiplication Warm-up

How to Make the Game:

1. Remove pages 1–20 from the Math Connections Games book.

2. Cut on the lines to make the 30 game cards and the envelope label.

3. Laminate the cards.

4. Glue the label to an envelope or place it inside a plastic portfolio.

5. Place game cards and the answer key (page 2) in the envelope. Store the originals for the reproducible pages (pages 19 and 20) in the envelope as well.

Directions:

1. Tell students they will be receiving a card which they should be ready to read aloud.

2. Pass out the cards randomly. Since there are 30 cards, some students may have more than one card.

3. Give students a few minutes to read over their cards.

4. On your signal, one student stands and reads his/her card.

5. Students solve the problems as they are read, and read their cards at the appropriate times. The game proceeds until every student has participated. The very last problem read in the game should have been answered by the number read to begin the game.

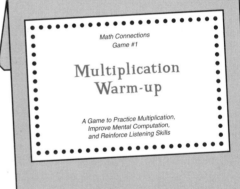

Math Connections
Game #1

Multiplication
Warm-up

A Game to Practice Multiplication, Improve Mental Computation, and Reinforce Listening Skills

Two reproducible activity pages are included with each Math Connections game. Use these pages to introduce the math skills before playing the game and to reinforce the skills after playing the game.

page 19

page 20

©2006 INCENTIVE PUBLICATIONS, Inc., Nashville, TN

MULTIPLICATION WARM-UP

Monitor student responses and prompt students, as necessary, through the game. You may choose a student monitor to be the prompter. This key represents the responses in one possible order.

In this game, any card may begin. Have the monitor choose the person to begin and find that person's card on the key using the small letter(s) on the upper left-hand corner of the card. The beginning reader will read only the black part (the question) on his or her card. The correct order will move down from that card, back up to the top, and then down to the starting card.

cc.	I have 360.	Where is 80 x 7?
aa.	I have 560.	Where is 2 x 90?
y.	I have 180.	Where is 60 x 5?
w.	I have 300.	Where is 500 x 8?
u.	I have 4,000.	Where is 7 x 100?
s.	I have 700.	Where is 9 x 500?
q.	I have 4,500.	Where is 80 x 80?
o.	I have 6,400.	Where is 7 x 60?
m.	I have 420.	Where is 30 x 7?
k.	I have 210.	Where is 5 x 900?
i.	I have 4,500.	Where is 40 x 80?
g.	I have 3,200.	Where is 60 x 10?
e.	I have 600.	Where is 70 x 6?
b.	I have 420.	Where is 50 x 40?
a.	I have 2,000.	Where is 80 x 11?
c.	I have 880.	Where is 9 x 90?
d.	I have 810.	Where is 500 x 5?
f.	I have 2,500.	Where is 6 x 90?
h.	I have 540.	Where is 70 x 7?
j.	I have 490.	Where is 40 x 40?
l.	I have 1,600.	Where is 30 x 5?
n.	I have 150.	Where is 70 x 4?
p.	I have 280.	Where is 9 x 80?
r.	I have 720.	Where is 40 x 6?
t.	I have 240.	Where is 22 x 20?
v.	I have 440.	Where is 90 x 3?
x.	I have 270.	Where is 7 x 50?
z.	I have 350.	Where is 60 x 8?
bb.	I have 480.	Where is 10 x 100?
dd.	I have 1,000.	Where is 40 x 9?

©2006 Incentive Publications, Inc., Nashville, TN

cc.

I have 360.

Where is 80 x 7?

aa.

I have 560.

Where is 2 x 90?

y.

I have 180.

Where is 60 x 5?

w.

I have 300.

Where is 500 x 8?

Multiplication Warm-up

Incentive Publications, Inc., Nashville, TN

Math Connections Game # 1

Multiplication Warm-up

Incentive Publications, Inc., Nashville, TN

Math Connections Game # 1

Multiplication Warm-up

Incentive Publications, Inc., Nashville, TN

Math Connections Game # 1

Multiplication Warm-up

Incentive Publications, Inc., Nashville, TN

Math Connections Game # 1

s.

I have 700.

Where is 9 x 500?

o.

I have 6,400.

Where is 7 x 60?

u.

I have 4,000.

Where is 7 x 100?

q.

I have 4,500.

Where is 80 x 80?

Multiplication Warm-up

Incentive Publications, Inc., Nashville, TN

Math Connections Game # 1

Multiplication Warm-up

Incentive Publications, Inc., Nashville, TN

Math Connections Game # 1

Multiplication Warm-up

Incentive Publications, Inc., Nashville, TN

Math Connections Game # 1

Multiplication Warm-up

Incentive Publications, Inc., Nashville, TN

Math Connections Game # 1

k.

I have 210.

Where is 5 x 900?

g.

I have 3,200.

Where is 60 x 10?

m.

I have 420.

Where is 30 x 7?

i.

I have 4,500.

Where is 40 x 80?

Multiplication
Warm-up

Incentive Publications, Inc., Nashville, TN

Multiplication
Warm-up

Incentive Publications, Inc., Nashville, TN

Multiplication
Warm-up

Incentive Publications, Inc., Nashville, TN

Multiplication
Warm-up

Incentive Publications, Inc., Nashville, TN

b.

I have 420.

Where is 50 x 40?

c.

I have 880.

Where is 9 x 90?

e.

I have 600.

Where is 70 x 6?

a.

I have 2,000.

Where is 80 x11?

Multiplication
Warm-up

Incentive Publications, Inc., Nashville, TN

Multiplication
Warm-up

Incentive Publications, Inc., Nashville, TN

Multiplication
Warm-up

Incentive Publications, Inc., Nashville, TN

Multiplication
Warm-up

Incentive Publications, Inc., Nashville, TN

d.

I have 810.

Where is 500 x 5?

f.

I have 2,500.

Where is 6 x 90?

h.

I have 540.

Where is 70 x 7?

j.

I have 490.

Where is 40 x 40?

Multiplication Warm-up

Incentive Publications, Inc., Nashville, TN

Multiplication Warm-up

Incentive Publications, Inc., Nashville, TN

Multiplication Warm-up

Incentive Publications, Inc., Nashville, TN

Multiplication Warm-up

Incentive Publications, Inc., Nashville, TN

n.

I have 150.

Where is 70 x 4?

r.

I have 720.

Where is 40 x 6?

l.

I have 1,600.

Where is 30 x 5?

p.

I have 280.

Where is 9 x 80?

Multiplication Warm-up

Incentive Publications, Inc., Nashville, TN

Multiplication Warm-up

Incentive Publications, Inc., Nashville, TN

Multiplication Warm-up

Incentive Publications, Inc., Nashville, TN

Multiplication Warm-up

Incentive Publications, Inc., Nashville, TN

v.

I have 440.
Where is 90 x 3?

z.

I have 350.
Where is 60 x 8?

t.

I have 240.
Where is 22 x 20?

x.

I have 270.
Where is 7 x 50?

Incentive Publications, Inc., Nashville, TN

Multiplication Warm-up

Math Connections Game # 1

Incentive Publications, Inc., Nashville, TN

Multiplication Warm-up

Math Connections Game # 1

Incentive Publications, Inc., Nashville, TN

Multiplication Warm-up

Math Connections Game # 1

Incentive Publications, Inc., Nashville, TN

Multiplication Warm-up

Math Connections Game # 1

bb.

I have 480.

Where is 10 x 100?

dd.

I have 1,000.

Where is 40 x 9?

Math Connections
Game #1

Multiplication Warm-up

A Game to Practice Multiplication,
Improve Mental Computation,
and Reinforce Listening Skills

Multiplication Warm-up

Incentive Publications, Inc., Nashville, TN

Multiplication Warm-up

Incentive Publications, Inc., Nashville, TN

Name _____

READ AND MULTIPLY

Solve the following problems. Show your work.

1. On Friday, there were twenty buses in line to pick up the students after school. Each bus had twelve rows of seats. In each row, two students sit on the left, and two students sit on the right. If every bus was loaded to capacity, how many students were riding the buses?

answer_____

2. The choir members helped set up the chairs in the auditorium before their concert. There were sixty rows of thirty chairs. How many chairs did the choir set up?

answer_____

3. Mr. Johnson grows and sells blueberries.The average blueberry bush has five hundred berries on it. There are two hundred bushes on his property. What is a good estimate of the number of berries Mr. Johnson will have?

answer_____

4. The school can drive will begin next week. Each advisory group hopes to secure 120 cans of nonperishable food for the food bank. If there are eight groups, how many cans is the school hoping to donate?

answer_____

5. The lunch lady serves pizza every Friday. There were 211 students that ordered pizza. She cooked 15 trays with 14 pieces of pizza in each tray. How many pieces of pizza did she cook?

answer_____

Did she have enough pizza for the students that Friday?

answer_____

6. The principal decided to buy candy bars for every student in the school. There were 527 students in his school. He went to the store and bought big boxes of candy bars to save money. There were 27 candy bars in each box. He bought 20 boxes of candy bars. Once he returned to school, he wondered if he had enough for everyone! How many candy bars did he buy?

answer_____

Did he have enough for each student?

answer_____

©2006 Incentive Publications, Inc., Nashville, TN

Math Connections Game #1

USE YOUR HEAD

Solve the following problems. Time yourself to see how fast you can complete all the problems.

1.   80 x 7 = _____

2.   2 x 90 = _____

3.   600 x 5 = _____

4.   5 x 80 = _____

5. 7,000 x 0 = _____

6.   10 x 90 = _____

7. 20 x 160 = _____

8. 20 x 500 = _____

9.   80 x 12 = _____

10. 700 x 10 = _____

11. 10 x 210 = _____

12.   11 x 40 = _____

13.   240 x 3 = _____

14.   13 x 40 = _____

15. 260 x 50 = _____

16. 300 x 60 = _____

17. 500 x 40 = _____

18. 170 x 80 = _____

19. 170 x 11 = _____

20. 13 x 120 = _____

21. 240 x 19 = _____

22. 41 x 150 = _____

23. 210 x 21 = _____

24. 27 x 140 = _____

©2006 Incentive Publications, Inc., Nashville, TN

Using the Language of Multiplication

How to Make the Game:

1. Remove pages 21–40 from Math Connections Games.

2. Cut on the lines to make the 30 game cards and the envelope label.

3. Laminate the cards.

4. Glue the label to an envelope or place it inside a plastic portfolio.

5. Place game cards and the answer key (page 22) in the envelope. Store the originals for the reproducible pages (pages 39 and 40) in the envelope as well.

Directions:

1. Tell students they will be receiving a card which they should be ready to read aloud.

2. Pass out the cards randomly. Since there are 30 cards, some students may have more than one card.

3. Give students a few minutes to read over their cards.

4. On your signal, one student stands and reads his/her card.

5. Students solve the problems as they are read, and read their cards at the appropriate times. The game proceeds until every student has participated. The very last problem read in the game should have been answered by the number read to begin the game.

Two reproducible activity pages are included with each Math Connections game. Use these pages to introduce the math skills before playing the game and to reinforce the skills after playing the game.

e. I have 81. Where is 2 x 2 x 2?

b. I have 8. Where is the value of twelve dimes?

a. I have $1.20. Where is a dozen dozens or a gross?

c. I have 144. Where is 1 x 10 x 2 x 30?

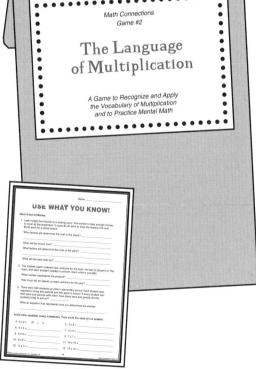

Math Connections Game #2

The Language of Multiplication

A Game to Recognize and Apply the Vocabulary of Multiplication and to Practice Mental Math

page 39

page 40

THE LANGUAGE OF MULTIPLICATION

Monitor student responses and prompt students, as necessary, through the game. You may choose a student monitor to be the prompter. This key represents the responses in one possible order.

In this game, any card may begin. Have the monitor choose the person to begin and find that person's card on the key using the small letter(s) on the upper left-hand corner of the card. The beginning reader will read only the black part (the question) on his or her card. The correct order will move down from that card, back up to the top, and then down to the starting card.

cc. I have 27. . . . . Where is 2^2?

aa. I have 4. . . . . Where is the product of 32 and 3?

y. I have 96. . . . . Where is 5 x 5 x 0?

w. I have 0. . . . . Where is two dozen?

u. I have 24. . . . . Where is 36 doubled?

s. I have 72. . . . . Where is the product of 11 and 2?

q. I have 22. . . . . Where is the product of 10 and 11?

o. I have 110. . . . . Where is 4^2?

m. I have 16. . . . . Where is 7^2?

k. I have 49. . . . . Where is 2 x 3 x 9?

i. I have 54. . . . . Where is 5^2?

g. I have 25. . . . . Where is 9 x 3 x 3?

e. I have 81. . . . . Where is 2 x 2 x 2?

b. I have 8. . . . . Where is the value of twelve dimes?

a. I have $1.20. . . . . Where is a dozen dozens or a gross?

c. I have 144. . . . . Where is 1 x 10 x 2 x 30?

d. I have 600. . . . . Where is 3 x 30 x 11?

f. I have 990. . . . . Where is the value of nineteen nickels?

h. I have 95 cents. . . . . Where is 2 x 3 x 11?

j. I have 66. . . . . Where is 8^2?

l. I have 64. . . . . Where is the value of forty dimes?

n. I have $4.00. . . . . Where is the product of the factors 20 and 13?

p. I have 260. . . . . Where is the value of sixty nickels?

r. I have $3.00. . . . . Where is 2^3 x 6?

t. I have 48. . . . . Where is the value of seventeen nickels?

v. I have 85 cents. . . . . Where is the product of the factors 20 and 40?

x. I have 800. . . . . Where is the value of fourteen quarters?

z. I have $3.50. . . . . Where is 2^2 x 9?

bb. I have 36. . . . . Where is 2 x 3^2 x 10?

dd. I have 180. . . . . Where is 3^3?

©2006 Incentive Publications, Inc., Nashville, TN

I have four.

Where is the product
of 32 and 3?

I have 0.

Where is two dozen?

I have 27.

Where is 2^2?

I have 96.

Where is 5 x 5 x 0?

The Language of Multiplication

Incentive Publications, Inc., Nashville, TN

Math Connections Game # 2

The Language of Multiplication

Incentive Publications, Inc., Nashville, TN

Math Connections Game # 2

The Language of Multiplication

Incentive Publications, Inc., Nashville, TN

Math Connections Game # 2

The Language of Multiplication

Incentive Publications, Inc., Nashville, TN

Math Connections Game # 2

s.

I have 72.

Where is the product of 11 and 2?

o.

I have 110.

Where is 4^2?

u.

I have 24.

Where is 36 doubled?

q.

I have 22.

Where is the product of 10 and 11?

The Language of Multiplication

Incentive Publications, Inc., Nashville, TN

The Language of Multiplication

Incentive Publications, Inc., Nashville, TN

The Language of Multiplication

Incentive Publications, Inc., Nashville, TN

The Language of Multiplication

Incentive Publications, Inc., Nashville, TN

k.

I have 49.

Where is 2 x 3 x 9?

g.

I have 25.

Where is 9 x 3 x 3?

m.

I have 16.

Where is 7^2?

i.

I have 54.

Where is 5^2?

The Language of Multiplication

Incentive Publications, Inc., Nashville, TN

The Language of Multiplication

Incentive Publications, Inc., Nashville, TN

The Language of Multiplication

Incentive Publications, Inc., Nashville, TN

The Language of Multiplication

Incentive Publications, Inc., Nashville, TN

b.

I have 8.

Where is the value
of twelve dimes?

c.

I have 144.

Where is 1 x 10 x 2 x 30?

e.

I have 81.

Where is 2 x 2 x 2?

a.

I have $1.20.

Where is a dozen dozens
or a gross?

The Language
of
Multiplication

Incentive Publications, Inc., Nashville, TN

The Language
of
Multiplication

Incentive Publications, Inc., Nashville, TN

Math Connections Game # 2

The Language
of
Multiplication

Incentive Publications, Inc., Nashville, TN

Math Connections Game # 2

The Language
of
Multiplication

Incentive Publications, Inc., Nashville, TN

Math Connections Game # 2

d.

I have 600.

Where is 3 x 30 x 11?

f.

I have 990.

Where is the value of nineteen nickels?

h.

I have 95 cents.

Where is 2 x 3 x 11?

j.

I have 66.

Where is 8^2?

The Language
of
Multiplication

Incentive Publications, Inc., Nashville, TN

The Language
of
Multiplication

Incentive Publications, Inc., Nashville, TN

The Language
of
Multiplication

Incentive Publications, Inc., Nashville, TN

The Language
of
Multiplication

Incentive Publications, Inc., Nashville, TN

n.

I have $4.00.

Where is the product of the factors 20 and 13?

r.

I have $3.00.

Where is 2^3 x 6?

l.

I have 64.

Where is the value of forty dimes?

p.

I have 260.

Where is the value of sixty nickels?

The Language of Multiplication

Incentive Publications, Inc., Nashville, TN

The Language of Multiplication

Incentive Publications, Inc., Nashville, TN

The Language of Multiplication

Incentive Publications, Inc., Nashville, TN

The Language of Multiplication

Incentive Publications, Inc., Nashville, TN

t.

I have 48.

Where is the value
of seventeen nickels?

---

v.

I have 85 cents.

Where is the product
of the factors 20 and 40?

---

x.

I have 800.

Where is the value
of fourteen quarters?

---

z.

I have $3.50.

Where is
$2^2 \times 9$?

The Language
of
Multiplication

Incentive Publications, Inc., Nashville, TN

The Language
of
Multiplication

Incentive Publications, Inc., Nashville, TN

The Language
of
Multiplication

Incentive Publications, Inc., Nashville, TN

The Language
of
Multiplication

Incentive Publications, Inc., Nashville, TN

bb.

I have 36.
Where is
$2 \times 3^2 \times 10$?

dd.

I have 180.
Where is 3^3?

Math Connections
Game #2

The Language of Multiplication

*A Game to Recognize and Apply
the Vocabulary of Multiplication
and to Practice Mental Math*

The Language
of
Multiplication

Incentive Publications, Inc., Nashville, TN

Math Connections Game # 2

The Language
of
Multiplication

Incentive Publications, Inc., Nashville, TN

Math Connections Game # 2

UNDERSTANDING THE TERMS

Tell how to solve each problem, then solve it.

1. If you double 5, what do you do?

    _____   _____

2. What does it mean to take 5 to the 2nd power?

    _____   _____

3. What is 8 squared?

    _____   _____

4. How do you solve the problem $3^2 \times 5$?

    _____   _____

5. How do you find the value of 40 nickels?

    _____   _____

6. Tell what you do to find the product of the factors 2, 8, and 9.

    _____   _____

7. How do you solve the problem $4^2 \times 5$?

    _____   _____

8. Tell what you do to find the product of the factors 2, 3^2, and 3.

    _____   _____

9. What does it mean to take 2 to the 3rd power?

    _____   _____

10. What is another way to write 7 to the 2nd power? How do you find the solution?

    _____   _____

11. How would you find 3^4?

    _____   _____

12. Tell how to find this product: 9×8^2.

    _____   _____

©2006 Incentive Publications, Inc., Nashville, TN   *Math Connections Game #2*

USE WHAT YOU KNOW!

Solve these problems.

1. Leah invited five friends to a skating party. She wanted to take enough money to cover all the expenses. It costs $4.50 each to enter the skating rink and $5.20 each for a pizza snack.

   What factors will determine the cost of the snack? _____

   _____

   What will the snack cost? _____

   What factors will determine the cost of the party? _____

   _____

   What will the total cost be? _____

2. The football coach ordered new uniforms for the team. He had 32 players on the team, and each student needed a uniform. Each uniform cost $65.

   What number represents the product? _____

   How much did he spend on team uniforms for the year? _____

3. There were 530 students at John's elementary school. Each student was required to bring two pencils and two pens to school. If every student had their pens and pencils with them, how many pens and pencils did the students bring to school? _____

   Write an equation that represents how you determined the answer.

   _____

Write each equation using exponents. Then write the value of the number.

4. 2 x 2 = 2^2 = 4   5. 3 x 3 = _____

6. 4 x 4 = _____   7. 5 x 5 = _____

8. 6 x 6 = _____   9. 7 x 7 = _____

10. 9 x 9 = _____   11. 10 x 10 = _____

12. 11 x 11 = _____   13. 12 x 12 = _____

©2006 Incentive Publications, Inc., Nashville, TN   *Math Connections Game #2*

Who Has the Problem?

How to Make the Game:

1. Remove pages 41–60 from Math Connections Games.

2. Cut on the lines to make the 30 game cards and the envelope label.

3. Laminate the cards.

4. Glue the label to an envelope or place it inside a plastic portfolio.

5. Place game cards and the answer key (page 42) in the envelope. Store the originals for the reproducible pages (pages 59 and 60) in the envelope as well.

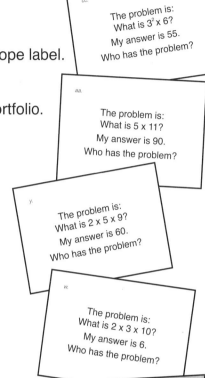

cc.
The problem is:
What is 3^2 x 6?
My answer is 55.
Who has the problem?

aa.
The problem is:
What is 5 x 11?
My answer is 90.
Who has the problem?

y.
The problem is:
What is 2 x 5 x 9?
My answer is 60.
Who has the problem?

w.
The problem is:
What is 2 x 3 x 10?
My answer is 6.
Who has the problem?

Directions:

1. Tell students they will be receiving a card which they should be ready to read aloud.

2. Pass out the cards randomly. Since there are 30 cards, some students may have more than one card.

3. Give students a few minutes to read over their cards.

4. On your signal, one student stands and reads his/her card.

5. Students solve the problems as they are read, and read their cards at the appropriate times. The game proceeds until every student has participated. The very last problem read in the game should have been answered by the number read to begin the game.

Two reproducible activity pages are included with each Math Connections game. Use these pages to introduce the math skills before playing the game and to reinforce the skills after playing the game.

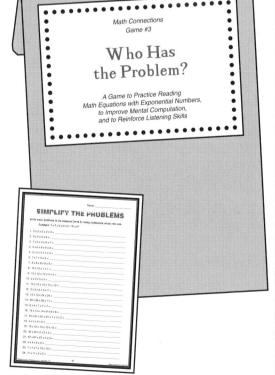

Math Connections
Game #3

Who Has
the Problem?

A Game to Practice Reading
Math Equations with Exponential Numbers,
to Improve Mental Computation,
and to Reinforce Listening Skills

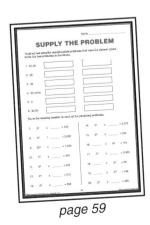

page 59

page 60

©2006 Incentive Publications, Inc., Nashville, TN

WHO HAS THE PROBLEM?

Monitor student responses and prompt students, as necessary, through the game. You may choose a student monitor to be the prompter. This key represents the responses in one possible order.

In this game, any card may begin. Have the monitor choose the person to begin and find that person's card on the key using the small letter(s) on the upper left-hand corner of the card. The beginning reader should read only the black part (My answer is __. Who has the problem?) on his or her card. The correct order will move down from that card, back up to the top, then down to the starting card.

cc.   The problem is: What is 3^2 x 6? My answer is 55. Who has the problem?

aa.   The problem is: What is 5 x 11? My answer is 90. Who has the problem?

y.   The problem is: What is 2 x 5 x 9? My answer is 60. Who has the problem?

w.   The problem is: What is 2 x 3 x 10? My answer is 6. Who has the problem?

u.   The problem is: What is 1 x 2 x 3? My answer is 12. Who has the problem?

s.   The problem is: What is 6 doubled? My answer is 24. Who has the problem?

q.   The problem is: What is 12 doubled. My answer is 48. Who has the problem?

o.   The problem is: What is 24 x 2? My answer is 140. Who has the problem?

m.   The problem is: What is the product of the factors 20 and 7? My answer is $1.00.
      Who has the problem?

k.   The problem is: What is the value of ten dimes? My answer is 36. Who has the problem?

i.   The problem is: What is 6^2? My answer is 72. Who has the problem?

g.   The problem is: What is 36 doubled? My answer is 49. Who has the problem?

e.   The problem is: What is 7^2? My answer is 4,000. Who has the problem?

b.   The problem is: What is the product of the factors 1, 20, and 200? My answer is 4.
      Who has the problem?

a.   The problem is: What is 2^2? My answer is 16. Who has the problem?

c.   The problem is: What is 2 x 2 x 2 x 2? My answer is 32. Who has the problem?

d.   The problem is: What is 16 doubled? My answer is 18. Who has the problem?

f.   The problem is: What is 2 x 3 x 3? My answer is 70. Who has the problem?

h.   The problem is: What is 2 x 5 x 7? My answer is 45. Who has the problem?

j.   The problem is: What is 3^2 x 5? My answer is $2.00. Who has the problem?

l.   The problem is: What is the value of forty nickels? My answer is 42. Who has the problem?

n.   The problem is: What is the product of the factors 2, 3, and 7? My answer is 50.
      Who has the problem?

p.   The problem is: What is 2 x 5^2? My answer is 28. Who has the problem?

r.   The problem is: What is 2^2 x 7? My answer is 56. Who has the problem?

t.   The problem is: What is 28 doubled? My answer is 25. Who has the problem?

v.   The problem is: What is 5 to the 2nd power? My answer is 81. Who has the problem?

x.   The problem is: What is 3^2 x 3^2? My answer is 44. Who has the problem?

z.   The problem is: What is 2^2 x 11? My answer is $15.00. Who has the problem?

bb.   The problem is: What is the value of 300 nickels? My answer is $30.00. Who has the problem?

dd.   The problem is: What is $15.00 doubled? My answer is 54. Who has the problem?

©2006 Incentive Publications, Inc., Nashville, TN

aa.

The problem is:
What is 5 x 11?

My answer is 90.

Who has the problem?

w.

The problem is:
What is 2 x 3 x 10?

My answer is 6.

Who has the problem?

cc.

The problem is:
What is 3^2 x 6?

My answer is 55.

Who has the problem?

y.

The problem is:
What is 2 x 5 x 9?

My answer is 60.

Who has the problem?

Who Has the Problem?

Incentive Publications, Inc., Nashville, TN

Who Has the Problem?

Incentive Publications, Inc., Nashville, TN

Who Has the Problem?

Incentive Publications, Inc., Nashville, TN

Who Has the Problem?

Incentive Publications, Inc., Nashville, TN

s.

The problem is:
What is 6 doubled?

My answer is 24.

Who has the problem?

---

o.

The problem is:
What is 24 x 2?

My answer is 140.

Who has the problem?

---

u.

The problem is:
What is 1 x 2 x 3?

My answer is 12.

Who has the problem?

---

q.

The problem is:
What is 12 doubled?

My answer is 48.

Who has the problem?

Incentive Publications, Inc., Nashville, TN

Who Has
the
Problem?

Incentive Publications, Inc., Nashville, TN

Who Has
the
Problem?

Math Connections Game # 3

Incentive Publications, Inc., Nashville, TN

Who Has
the
Problem?

Incentive Publications, Inc., Nashville, TN

Who Has
the
Problem?

k.

The problem is:
What is the value
of ten dimes?

My answer is 36.

Who has the problem?

g.

The problem is:
What is 36 doubled?

My answer is 49.

Who has the problem?

m.

The problem is:
What is the product of
the factors 20 and 7?

My answer is $1.00.

Who has the problem?

i.

The problem is:
What is 6^2?

My answer is 72.

Who has the problem?

Who Has the Problem?

Incentive Publications, Inc., Nashville, TN

Who Has the Problem?

Incentive Publications, Inc., Nashville, TN

Who Has the Problem?

Incentive Publications, Inc., Nashville, TN

Who Has the Problem?

Incentive Publications, Inc., Nashville, TN

b.

The problem is:
What is the product of
the factors 1, 20, and 2000?

My answer is 4.

Who has the problem?

c.

The problem is:
What is 2 x 2 x 2 x 2?

My answer is 32.

Who has the problem?

e.

The problem is:
What is 7^2?

My answer is 4,000.

Who has the problem?

a.

The problem is:
What is 2^2?

My answer is 16.

Who has the problem?

Incentive Publications, Inc., Nashville, TN

Who Has
the
Problem?

Math Connections Game # 3

Incentive Publications, Inc., Nashville, TN

Who Has
the
Problem?

Math Connections Game # 3

Incentive Publications, Inc., Nashville, TN

Who Has
the
Problem?

Math Connections Game # 3

Incentive Publications, Inc., Nashville, TN

Who Has
the
Problem?

Math Connections Game # 3

d.

The problem is:
What is 16 doubled?

My answer is 18.
Who has the problem?

f.

The problem is:
What is 2 x 3 x 3?

My answer is 70.
Who has the problem?

h.

The problem is:
What is 2 x 5 x 7?

My answer is 45.
Who has the problem?

j.

The problem is:
What is 3^2 x 5?

My answer is $2.00.
Who has the problem?

Incentive Publications, Inc., Nashville, TN

Who Has the Problem?

Incentive Publications, Inc., Nashville, TN

Who Has the Problem?

Incentive Publications, Inc., Nashville, TN

Who Has the Problem?

Incentive Publications, Inc., Nashville, TN

Who Has the Problem?

n.

The problem is:
What is the product of
the factors 2, 3, and 7?

My answer is 50.

Who has the problem?

r.

The problem is:
What is 2^2 x 7?

My answer is 56.

Who has the problem?

l.

The problem is:
What is the value
of forty nickels?

My answer is 42.

Who has the problem?

p.

The problem is:
What is 2×5^2?

My answer is 28.

Who has the problem?

Incentive Publications, Inc., Nashville, TN

Who Has
the
Problem?

Incentive Publications, Inc., Nashville, TN

Who Has
the
Problem?

Incentive Publications, Inc., Nashville, TN

Who Has
the
Problem?

Incentive Publications, Inc., Nashville, TN

Who Has
the
Problem?

t.

The problem is:
What is 28 doubled?

My answer is 25.

Who has the problem?

v.

The problem is:
What is 5 to the 2nd power?

My answer is 81.

Who has the problem?

x.

The problem is:
What is $3^2 \times 3^2$?

My answer is 44.

Who has the problem?

z.

The problem is:
What is $2^2 \times 11$?

My answer is $15.00.

Who has the problem?

Who Has the Problem?

Incentive Publications, Inc., Nashville, TN

Who Has the Problem?

Incentive Publications, Inc., Nashville, TN

Who Has the Problem?

Incentive Publications, Inc., Nashville, TN

Who Has the Problem?

Incentive Publications, Inc., Nashville, TN

bb.

The problem is:
What is the value of
300 nickels?

My answer is $30.00.
Who has the problem?

dd.

The problem is:
What is $15.00 doubled?

My answer is 54.
Who has the problem?

Math Connections
Game #3

Who Has
the Problem?

A Game to Practice Reading
Math Equations with Exponential Numbers,
to Improve Mental Computation,
and to Reinforce Listening Skills

Incentive Publications, Inc., Nashville, TN

Who Has the Problem?

Incentive Publications, Inc., Nashville, TN

Who Has the Problem?

Name _____

SUPPLY THE PROBLEM

Think of two possible multiplication problems that have the answer given. Write the two problems in the boxes.

1. $1.00

2. 56

3. 36

4. 65 cents

5. 0

6. $3.00

Fill in the missing number in each of the following problems.

7. 3^3 x _____ = 432

8. 5^3 x _____ = 2,000

9. 25^2 x _____ = 1,250

10. 7^3 x _____ = 343

11. 9^2 x _____ = 243

12. 4^4 x _____ = 512

13. 2^5 x _____ = 256

14. 5^5 x _____ = 9,375

15. 9^2 x _____ = 324

16. _____ x 6^2 = 144

17. 7^3 x _____ = 3,430

18. _____ x 2^2 = 56

19. _____ x 2^3 = 168

20. 2^4 x _____ = 320

59

©2006 Incentive Publications, Inc., Nashville, TN

Math Connections Game #3

SIMPLIFY THE PROBLEMS

Write each problem in its simplest form by using exponents when you can.

Example: $4 \times 4 \times 6 \times 6 \times 6 = 4^2 \times 6^3$

1. $2 \times 2 \times 2 \times 2 \times 3 =$ _____

2. $5 \times 5 \times 5 \times 6 =$ _____

3. $7 \times 3 \times 3 \times 9 \times 7 =$ _____

4. $3 \times 6 \times 6 \times 6 \times 6 =$ _____

5. $2 \times 2 \times 4 \times 4 \times 4 =$ _____

6. $7 \times 7 \times 5 \times 5 =$ _____

7. $8 \times 8 \times 8 \times 9 \times 9 =$ _____

8. $10 \times 10 \times 1 \times 1 =$ _____

9. $12 \times 12 \times 12 \times 4 \times 4 =$ _____

10. $2 \times 2 \times 5 \times 5 =$ _____

11. $15 \times 15 \times 15 \times 15 \times 12 =$ _____

12. $3 \times 3 \times 3 \times 3 \times 7 =$ _____

13. $13 \times 13 \times 24 \times 24 =$ _____

14. $58 \times 58 \times 58 \times 17 =$ _____

15. $6 \times 6 \times 7 \times 7 \times 7 =$ _____

16. $14 \times 14 \times 14 \times 8 \times 8 \times 8 =$ _____

17. $81 \times 81 \times 81 \times 81 \times 7 \times 2 \times 2 =$ _____

18. $5 \times 5 \times 9 \times 9 =$ _____

19. $10 \times 10 \times 13 \times 13 \times 13 =$ _____

20. $34 \times 34 \times 2 \times 2 \times 2 =$ _____

21. $67 \times 67 \times 67 \times 3 \times 3 =$ _____

22. $4 \times 4 \times 9 \times 9 =$ _____

23. $7 \times 7 \times 7 \times 19 \times 19 =$ _____

24. $11 \times 11 \times 5 \times 5 =$ _____

©2006 INCENTIVE PUBLICATIONS, Inc., Nashville, TN

Math Connections Game #3

Division Warm-up

How to Make the Game:

1. Remove pages 61–80 from the Math Connections Games book.

2. Cut on the lines to make the 30 game cards and the envelope label.

3. Laminate the cards.

4. Glue the label to an envelope or place it inside a plastic portfolio.

5. Place game cards and the Answer Key (page 62) in the envelope. Store the originals for the reproducible pages (pages 79 and 80) in the envelope as well.

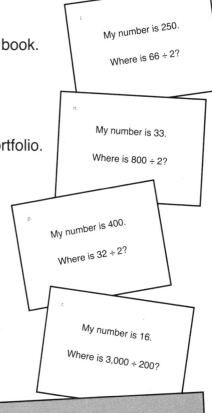

Directions:

1. Tell students they will be receiving a card which they should be ready to read aloud.

2. Pass out the cards randomly. Since there are 30 cards, some students may have more than one card.

3. Give students a few minutes to read over their cards.

4. On your signal, one student stands and reads his/her card.

5. Students solve the problems as they are read, and read their cards at the appropriate times. The game proceeds until every student has participated. The very last problem read in the game should have been answered by the number read to begin the game.

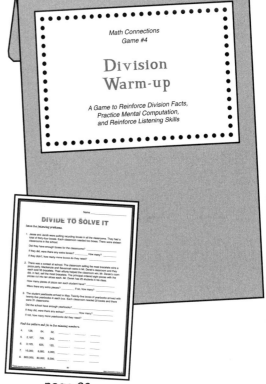

Two reproducible activity pages are included with each Math Connections game. Use these pages to introduce the math skills before playing the game and to reinforce the skills after playing the game.

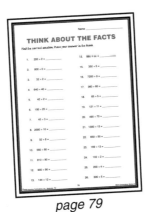

page 79

page 80

©2006 Incentive Publications, Inc., Nashville, TN

DIVISION WARM-UP

Monitor student responses and prompt students, as necessary, through the game. You may choose a student monitor to be the prompter. This key represents the responses in one possible order.

In this game, any card may begin. Have the monitor choose the person to begin and find that person's card on the key using the small letter(s) on the upper left-hand corner of the card. The beginning reader should read only the black part (the question) on his or her card. The correct order will move down from that card, back up to the top, and then down to the starting card.

cc.	My number is 35.	. . . .	Where is 200 ÷ 2?
aa.	My number is 100.	. . . .	Where is 90 ÷ 3?
y.	My number is 30.	. . . .	Where is 100 ÷ 2?
w.	My number is 50.	. . . .	Where is 33 ÷ 3?
u.	My number is 11.	. . . .	Where is 36 ÷ 2?
s.	My number is 18.	. . . .	Where is 90 ÷ 3?
q.	My number is 30.	. . . .	Where is 200 ÷ 5?
o.	My number is 40.	. . . .	Where is 210 ÷ 3?
m.	My number is 70.	. . . .	Where is 810 ÷ 9?
k.	My number is 90.	. . . .	Where is 6,000 ÷ 3?
i.	My number is 2,000.	. . . .	Where is 340 ÷ 2?
g.	My number is 170.	. . . .	Where is 660 ÷ 3?
e.	My number is 220.	. . . .	Where is 420 ÷ 2?
b.	My number is 210.	. . . .	Where is 260 ÷ 2?
a.	My number is 130.	. . . .	Where is 2,400 ÷ 4?
c.	My number is 600.	. . . .	Where is 2,400 ÷ 2?
d.	My number is 1,200.	. . . .	Where is 600 ÷ 30?
f.	My number is 20.	. . . .	Where is 160 ÷ 20?
h.	My number is 8.	. . . .	Where is 62 ÷ 2?
j.	My number is 31.	. . . .	Where is 500 ÷ 2?
l.	My number is 250.	. . . .	Where is 66 ÷ 2?
n.	My number is 33.	. . . .	Where is 800 ÷ 2?
p.	My number is 400.	. . . .	Where is 32 ÷ 2?
r.	My number is 16.	. . . .	Where is 3,000 ÷ 200?
t.	My number is 15.	. . . .	Where is 120 ÷ 2?
v.	My number is 60.	. . . .	Where is 2,000 ÷ 200?
x.	My number is 10.	. . . .	Where is 700 ÷ 0?
z.	My number is 0.	. . . .	Where is 120 ÷ 30?
bb.	My number is 4.	. . . .	Where is 10,000 ÷ 2?
dd.	My number is 5,000.	. . . .	Where is 700 ÷ 20?

©2006 Incentive Publications, Inc., Nashville, TN

aa.

My number is 100.

Where is 90 ÷ 3?

w.

My number is 50.

Where is 33 ÷ 3?

cc.

My number is 35.

Where is 200 ÷ 2?

y.

My number is 30.

Where is 100 ÷ 2?

Incentive Publications, Inc., Nashville, TN

Division
Warm-up

Math Connections Game # 4

Incentive Publications, Inc., Nashville, TN

Division
Warm-up

Math Connections Game # 4

Incentive Publications, Inc., Nashville, TN

Division
Warm-up

Math Connections Game # 4

Incentive Publications, Inc., Nashville, TN

Division
Warm-up

Math Connections Game # 4

s.

My number is 18.

Where is 90 ÷ 3?

o.

My number is 40.

Where is 210 ÷ 3?

u.

My number is 11.

Where is 36 ÷ 2?

q.

My number is 30.

Where is 200 ÷ 5?

Division
Warm-up

Incentive Publications, Inc., Nashville, TN

Division
Warm-up

Incentive Publications, Inc., Nashville, TN

Division
Warm-up

Incentive Publications, Inc., Nashville, TN

Division
Warm-up

Incentive Publications, Inc., Nashville, TN

k.

My number is 90.

Where is 6,000 ÷ 3?

g.

My number is 170.

Where is 660 ÷ 3?

m.

My number is 70.

Where is 810 ÷ 9?

i.

My number is 2,000.

Where is 340 ÷ 2?

Incentive Publications, Inc., Nashville, TN

Division
Warm-up

Incentive Publications, Inc., Nashville, TN

Division
Warm-up

Incentive Publications, Inc., Nashville, TN

Division
Warm-up

Incentive Publications, Inc., Nashville, TN

Division
Warm-up

b.

My number is 210.

Where is 260 ÷ 2?

c.

My number is 600.

Where is 2,400 ÷ 2?

e.

My number is 220.

Where is 420 ÷ 2?

a.

My number is 130.

Where is 2,400 ÷ 4?

Incentive Publications, Inc., Nashville, TN

Division
Warm-up

Incentive Publications, Inc., Nashville, TN

Division
Warm-up

Incentive Publications, Inc., Nashville, TN

Division
Warm-up

Incentive Publications, Inc., Nashville, TN

Division
Warm-up

d.

My number is 1,200.

Where is 600 ÷ 30?

f.

My number is 20.

Where is 160 ÷ 20?

h.

My number is 8.

Where is 62 ÷ 2?

j.

My number is 31.

Where is 500 ÷ 2?

Division
Warm-up

Incentive Publications, Inc., Nashville, TN

Math Connections Game # 4

Division
Warm-up

Incentive Publications, Inc., Nashville, TN

Math Connections Game # 4

Division
Warm-up

Incentive Publications, Inc., Nashville, TN

Math Connections Game # 4

Division
Warm-up

Incentive Publications, Inc., Nashville, TN

Math Connections Game # 4

n.

My number is 33.

Where is 800 ÷ 2?

r.

My number is 16.

Where is 3,000 ÷ 200?

l.

My number is 250.

Where is 66 ÷ 2?

p.

My number is 400.

Where is 32 ÷ 2?

Division
Warm-up

Incentive Publications, Inc., Nashville, TN

Division
Warm-up

Incentive Publications, Inc., Nashville, TN

Division
Warm-up

Incentive Publications, Inc., Nashville, TN

Division
Warm-up

Incentive Publications, Inc., Nashville, TN

t.

My number is 15.

Where is 120 ÷ 2?

v.

My number is 60.

Where is 2,000 ÷ 200?

x.

My number is 10.

Where is 700 ÷ 0?

z.

My number is 0.

Where is 120 ÷ 30?

Incentive Publications, Inc., Nashville, TN

Division
Warm-up

Incentive Publications, Inc., Nashville, TN

Division
Warm-up

Incentive Publications, Inc., Nashville, TN

Division
Warm-up

Incentive Publications, Inc., Nashville, TN

Division
Warm-up

bb.

My number is 4.

Where is 10,000 ÷ 2?

dd.

My number is 5,000.

Where is 700 ÷ 20?

Math Connections
Game #4

Division
Warm-up

A Game to Reinforce Division Facts,
Practice Mental Computation,
and Reinforce Listening Skills

Incentive Publications, Inc., Nashville, TN

Division
Warm-up

Math Connections Game # 4

Incentive Publications, Inc., Nashville, TN

Division
Warm-up

Math Connections Game # 4

THINK ABOUT THE FACTS

Find the correct solution. Place your answer in the blank.

1. $200 \div 2 =$ _____

2. $900 \div 0 =$ _____

3. $32 \div 2 =$ _____

4. $640 \div 40 =$ _____

5. $42 \div 2 =$ _____

6. $100 \div 25 =$ _____

7. $45 \div 3 =$ _____

8. $2000 \div 10 =$ _____

9. $32 \div 8 =$ _____

10. $560 \div 80 =$ _____

11. $810 \div 90 =$ _____

12. $900 \div 90 =$ _____

13. $144 \div 12 =$ _____

14. $660 \div 60 =$ _____

15. $350 \div 5 =$ _____

16. $7200 \div 9 =$ _____

17. $360 \div 60 =$ _____

18. $65 \div 5 =$ _____

19. $121 \div 11 =$ _____

20. $490 \div 70 =$ _____

21. $1300 \div 13 =$ _____

22. $650 \div 50 =$ _____

23. $169 \div 13 =$ _____

24. $102 \div 2 =$ _____

25. $200 \div 4 =$ _____

26. $300 \div 5 =$ _____

©2006 Incentive Publications, Inc., Nashville, TN

Math Connections Game #4

Name _____

DIVIDE TO SOLVE IT

Solve the following problems.

1. Jesse and Jacob were putting recycling boxes in all the classrooms. They had a total of thirty-four boxes. Each classroom needed two boxes. There were sixteen classrooms in the school.

   Did they have enough boxes for the classrooms? _____

   If they did, were there any extra boxes? _____ How many? _____

   If they didn't, how many more boxes do they need? _____

2. There was a contest at school. The classroom selling the most bracelets wins a pizza party. Mackenzie and Savannah were in Mr. Derek's classroom and they each sold 55 bracelets. Their efforts helped the classroom win; Mr. Derek's room did, in fact, sell the most bracelets. The principal ordered eight pizzas with the pizzas cut into ten slices each. Mr. Derek has 25 students in his class.

   How many pieces of pizza can each student have? _____

   Were there any extra pieces? _____ If so, how many? _____

3. The student yearbooks arrived in May. Twenty-five boxes of yearbooks arrived with twenty-five yearbooks in each box. Each classroom needed 20 books and there were 31 classrooms.

   Did the school have enough yearbooks?_____

   If they did, were there any extras? _____ How many? _____

   If not, how many more yearbooks did they need? _____

Find the pattern and fill in the missing numbers.

4.   128,   64,   32,   _____ ,   _____ ,   _____

5.   2,187,   729,   243,   _____ ,   _____ ,   _____

6.   3,125,   625,   125,   _____ ,   _____ ,   _____

7.   16,000, 8,000,   4,000,   _____ ,   _____ ,   _____

8.   800,000, 80,000, 8,000,   _____ ,   _____ ,   _____

©2006 Incentive Publications, Inc., Nashville, TN

Math Connections Game #4

Give Me Half!

How to Make the Game:

1. Remove pages 81–100 from Math Connections Games.

2. Cut on the lines to make the 30 game cards and the envelope label.

3. Laminate the cards.

4. Glue the label to an envelope or place it inside a plastic portfolio.

5. Place game cards and the Answer Key (page 82) in the envelope. Store the originals for the reproducible pages (pages 99 and 100) in the envelope as well.

Directions:

1. Tell students they will be receiving a card which they should be ready to read aloud.

2. Pass out the cards randomly. Since there are 30 cards, some students may have more than one card.

3. Give students a few minutes to read over their cards.

4. On your signal, one student stands and reads his/her card.

5. Students solve the problems as they are read, and read their cards at the appropriate times. The game proceeds until every student has participated.

Two reproducible activity pages are included with each Math Connections game. Use these pages to introduce the math skills before playing the game and to reinforce the skills after playing the game.

You are going to start the game. Stand up and read:

Let's begin with a nice big number—562,000,000,000. Somebody, give me half!

My number is 281,000,000,000.

Give me half!

My number is 14,500,000,000.

Give me half!

My number is 70,250,000,000.

Give me half!

Math Connections
Game #5

Give Me
Half!

A Game to Practice Reading Large Numbers,
Estimating Halves,
and Reinforcing Listening Skills

page 99

page 100

GIVE ME HALF!

Monitor student responses and prompt students, as necessary, through the game. You may choose a student monitor to be the prompter. This key represents the responses in order. The student with the beginning card stands up and reads his/her card. Before beginning, remind students to use their estimating skills.

1. Let's begin with a nice big number—562,000,000,000. Somebody, give me half!

2. My number is 281,000,000,000. Give me half!

3. My number is 14,500,000,000. Give me half!

4. My number is 70,250,000,000. Give me half!

5. My number is 35,125,000,000. Give me half!

6. My number is 17,562,500,000. Give me half!

7. My number is 8,781,250,000. Give me half!

8. My number is 4,390,625,000. Give me half!

9. My number is 2,195,312,500. Give me half!

10. My number is 1,097,656,200. Give me half!

11. My number is 548,828,100. Give me half!

12. My number is 274,414,050. Give me half!

13. My number is 137,207,020. Give me half!

14. My number is 68,603,510. Give me half!

15. My number is 34,301,755. Give me half!

16. My number is 17,150,877. Give me half!

17. My number is 8,574,385. Give me half!

18. My number is 4,287,192.5. Give me half!

19. My number is 2,143,596.2. Give me half!

20. My number is 1,071,798.1. Give me half!

21. My number is 535,899.05. Give me half!

22. My number is 267,949.52. Give me half!

23. My number is 133,974.76. Give me half!

24. My number is 66,987.38. Give me half!

25. My number is 33,493.69. Give me half!

26. My number is 16,746.845. Give me half!

27. My number is 8, 373.4225. Give me half!

28. My number is 4,186.7112. Give me half!

29. My number is 2,093.3556. Give me half!

30. My number is 1,046.6778. That's 562 trillion halved 29 times! I "half" had enough! How about you?

©2006 Incentive Publications, Inc., Nashville, TN

You are going to start the game. Stand up and read:

Let's begin with a nice big number—562,000,000,000. Somebody, give me half!

My number is 14,500,000,000.

Give me half!

My number is 281,000,000,000.

Give me half!

My number is 70,250,000,000.

Give me half!

Incentive Publications, Inc., Nashville, TN

Give Me
Half!

Incentive Publications, Inc., Nashville, TN

Give Me
Half!

Incentive Publications, Inc., Nashville, TN

Give Me
Half!

Incentive Publications, Inc., Nashville, TN

Give Me
Half!

My number is
17,562,500,000.

Give me half!

My number is
4,390,625,000.

Give me half!

My number is
35,125,000,000.

Give me half!

My number is
8,781,250,000.

Give me half!

Incentive Publications, Inc., Nashville, TN

Give Me Half!

Incentive Publications, Inc., Nashville, TN

Give Me Half!

Incentive Publications, Inc., Nashville, TN

Give Me Half!

Incentive Publications, Inc., Nashville, TN

Give Me Half!

My number is
1,097,656,200.

Give me half!

My number is
274,414,050.

Give me half!

My number is
2,195,312,500.

Give me half!

My number is
548,828,100.

Give me half!

Incentive Publications, Inc., Nashville, TN

Give Me Half!

Incentive Publications, Inc., Nashville, TN

Give Me Half!

Incentive Publications, Inc., Nashville, TN

Give Me Half!

Incentive Publications, Inc., Nashville, TN

Give Me Half!

My number is 68,603,510.

Give me half!

My number is 17,150,877.

Give me half!

My number is 137,207,020.

Give me half!

My number is 34,301,755.

Give me half!

Incentive Publications, Inc., Nashville, TN

Give Me Half!

Incentive Publications, Inc., Nashville, TN

Give Me Half!

Incentive Publications, Inc., Nashville, TN

Give Me Half!

Incentive Publications, Inc., Nashville, TN

Give Me Half!

My number is 4,287,192.5.

Give me half!

My number is 1,071,798.1.

Give me half!

My number is 8,574,385.

Give me half!

My number is 2,143,596.2.

Give me half!

Incentive Publications, Inc., Nashville, TN

Give Me Half!

Incentive Publications, Inc., Nashville, TN

Give Me Half!

Incentive Publications, Inc., Nashville, TN

Give Me Half!

Incentive Publications, Inc., Nashville, TN

Give Me Half!

My number is 535,899.05.

Give me half!

My number is 267,949.52.

Give me half!

My number is 133,974.76.

Give me half!

My number is 66,987.38.

Give me half!

Incentive Publications, Inc., Nashville, TN

Give Me Half!

Incentive Publications, Inc., Nashville, TN

Give Me Half!

Incentive Publications, Inc., Nashville, TN

Give Me Half!

Incentive Publications, Inc., Nashville, TN

Give Me Half!

My number is 16,746.845.

Give me half!

My number is 4,186.7112.

Give me half!

My number is 33,493.69.

Give me half!

My number is 8,373.4225.

Give me half!

Incentive Publications, Inc., Nashville, TN

Give Me
Half!

Incentive Publications, Inc., Nashville, TN

Give Me
Half!

Incentive Publications, Inc., Nashville, TN

Give Me
Half!

Incentive Publications, Inc., Nashville, TN

Give Me
Half!

My number is 2,093.3556.

Give me half!

My number is 1,046.6778.

That's 562 trillion halved 29 times!

I "half" had enough! How about you?

Math Connections
Game #5

Give Me Half!

A Game to Practice Reading Large Numbers,
Estimating Halves,
and Reinforcing Listening Skills

Incentive Publications, Inc., Nashville, TN

Give Me Half!

Incentive Publications, Inc., Nashville, TN

Give Me Half!

ESTIMATE ONE-HALF

To estimate means to make a reasonable guess. Estimation is a good tool to use when you do not need to end up with a precise count or answer, or to see if a given answer is reasonable. Rounding is helpful when you estimate.

For example, if you need to find half of 382,956, think: half of 400,000 is 200,000, so the answer will have to be a little less than 200,000. It will not be close to 20,000 or 2,000.

Estimate to choose the correct answer, then solve the problem to prove you were accurate.

1. What is half of 896,436?
   a. 4,482
   b. 448,218
   c. 44,821
   d. 4,482,180

   Solve it.

2. What is half of 38,492,534?
   a. 1,924,626
   b. 192,462,670
   c. 19,246,267
   d. 19,246

   Solve it.

3. What is half of 2,612?
   a. 13, 060
   b. 130
   c. 1.36
   d. 1,306

   Solve it.

4. What is half of 53,826,713,800?
   a. 26,913
   b. 26,913,256
   c. 26,913,256,900
   d. 2,691,325,690

   Solve it.

5. What is half of 186.24?
   a. 93.12
   b. 9,312
   c. 9.312
   d. 931.2

   Solve it.

6. What is half of 46.20?
   a. 2,310
   b. 231
   c. 23.10
   d. 2.310

   Solve it.

7. What is half of 6,351,892?
   a. 31,759
   b. 31,759,460
   c. 317,594
   d. 3,175,946

   Solve it.

8. What is half of 46.28642?
   a. 2.314321
   b. 23.14321
   c. 231.4321
   d. 2,314.321

   Solve it.

©2006 Incentive Publications, Inc., Nashville, TN

Name _____

BIG NUMBERS

Write these numbers in words.

1. 2,783,726 _____

2. 71,322,564 _____

3. 893,482,108 _____

4. 72,943,740,524 _____

5. 8,347,931,720,640 _____

Write these numbers in standard form.

6. Two million, eight hundred thirty-nine thousand, five hundred eleven and three tenths

   _____

7. One trillion, seven hundred forty-four million, one hundred twenty-four thousand

   _____

8. Three million, seven hundred eleven thousand, forty-three

   _____

9. Eight hundred thousand, ten and forty-five hundreths

   _____

10. One million, nine hundred seventy-two thousand, nine hundred sixty-one

    _____

Answer each question to show you understand place value.

11. In one year, Tiger Woods received $60,000,000.00 in sports endorsement contracts. What is the value of the 6 in this large number? _____

12. Another professional golfer, Mark Brooks, made $1,430,000.00 in one year. What is the value of the 4 in his earnings? _____

13. Before he retired, Michael Jordan received $25,000,000.00 for a one-year deal. What digit is in the ten millions place in this figure? _____

14. A player negoitiates a three-year extension of his contract for $10,250,000. What is the value of the 5 in his earnings? _____

©2006 Incentive Publications, Inc., Nashville, TN

Divide and Conquer

How to Make the Game:

1. Remove pages 101–120 from the Math Connections Games book.

2. Cut on the lines to make the 30 game cards and the envelope label.

3. Laminate the cards.

4. Glue the label to an envelope or place it inside a plastic portfolio.

5. Place game cards and the Answer Key (page 102) in the envelope. Store the originals for the reproducible pages (pages 119 and 120) in the envelope as well.

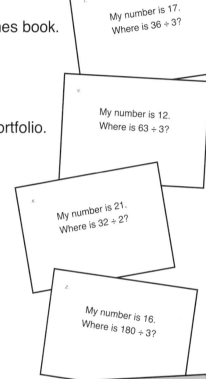

t.
My number is 17.
Where is 36 ÷ 3?

v.
My number is 12.
Where is 63 ÷ 3?

x.
My number is 21.
Where is 32 ÷ 2?

z.
My number is 16.
Where is 180 ÷ 3?

Directions:

1. Tell students they will be receiving a card which they should be ready to read aloud.

2. Pass out the cards randomly. Since there are 30 cards, some students may have more than one card.

3. Give students a few minutes to read over their cards.

4. On your signal, one student stands and reads his/her card.

5. Students solve the problems as they are read, and read their cards at the appropriate times. The game proceeds until every student has participated. The very last problem read in the game should have been answered by the number read to begin the game.

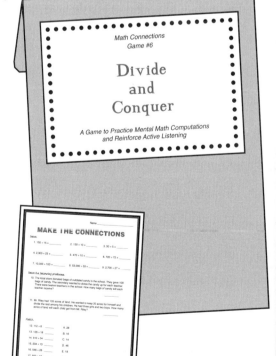

Math Connections
Game #6

Divide
and
Conquer

A Game to Practice Mental Math Computations and Reinforce Active Listening

Two reproducible activity pages are included with each Math Connections game. Use these pages to introduce the math skills before playing the game and to reinforce the skills after playing the game.

page 119

page 120

©2006 INCENTIVE PUBLICATIONS, Inc., Nashville, TN

DIVIDE AND CONQUER

Monitor student responses and prompt students, as necessary, through the game. You may choose a student monitor to be the prompter. This key represents the responses in one possible order.

In this game, any card may begin. Have the monitor choose the person to begin and find that person's card on the key using the small letter(s) on the upper left-hand corner of the card. The beginning reader will read only the black part (the question) on his or her card. The correct order will move down from that card, back up to the top, and then down to the starting card. If played correctly, all students will have read their card aloud, and the last student to say "My Number is . . ." will be the student that started the game.

cc.	My number is 35.	Where is 100 ÷ 25?
aa.	My number is 4.	Where is 0 ÷ 100?
y.	My number is 0.	Where is 45 ÷ 3?
w.	My number is 15.	Where is 32 ÷ 32?
u.	My number is 1.	Where is 100 ÷ 4?
s.	My number is 25.	Where is 93 ÷ 3?
q.	My number is 31.	Where is 48 ÷ 6?
o.	My number is 8.	Where is 100 ÷ 20?
m.	My number is 5.	Where is 1000 ÷ 10?
k	My number is 100.	Where is 500 ÷ 10?
i.	My number is 50.	Where is 54 ÷ 6?
g.	My number is 9.	Where is 120 ÷ 4?
e.	My number is 30.	Where is 49 ÷ 7?
b.	My number is 7.	Where is 39 ÷ 3?
a.	My number is 13.	Where is 48 ÷ 8?
c.	My number is 6.	Where is 100 ÷ 5?
d.	My number is 20.	Where is 200 ÷ 5?
f.	My number is 40.	Where is 99 ÷ 3?
h.	My number is 33.	Where is 180 ÷ 10?
j.	My number is 18.	Where is 50 ÷ 5?
l.	My number is 10.	Where is 44 ÷ 4?
n.	My number is 11.	Where is 26 ÷ 13?
p.	My number is 2.	Where is 88 ÷ 4?
r.	My number is 22.	Where is 51 ÷ 3?
t.	My number is 17.	Where is 36 ÷ 3?
v.	My number is 12.	Where is 63 ÷ 3?
x	My number is 21.	Where is 32 ÷ 2?
z.	My number is 16.	Where is 180 ÷ 3?
bb.	My number is 60.	Where is 30 ÷ 10?
dd.	My number is 3.	Where is 70 ÷ 2?

©2006 Incentive Publications, Inc., Nashville, TN

My number is 4.

Where is 0 ÷ 100?

aa.

My number is 15.

Where is 32 ÷ 32?

w.

My number is 35.

Where is 100 ÷ 25?

cc.

My number is 0.

Where is 45 ÷ 3?

y.

Incentive Publications, Inc., Nashville, TN

Divide
and
Conquer

Incentive Publications, Inc., Nashville, TN

Divide
and
Conquer

Incentive Publications, Inc., Nashville, TN

Divide
and
Conquer

Incentive Publications, Inc., Nashville, TN

Divide
and
Conquer

My number is 25.
Where is 93 ÷ 3?

My number is 8.
Where is 100 ÷ 20?

My number is 1.
Where is 100 ÷ 4?

My number is 31.
Where is 48 ÷ 6?

Incentive Publications, Inc., Nashville, TN

Divide
and
Conquer

Incentive Publications, Inc., Nashville, TN

Divide
and
Conquer

Incentive Publications, Inc., Nashville, TN

Divide
and
Conquer

Incentive Publications, Inc., Nashville, TN

Divide
and
Conquer

k.

My number is 100.
Where is 500 ÷ 10?

g.

My number is 9.
Where is 120 ÷ 4?

m.

My number is 5.
Where is 1000 ÷ 10?

i.

My number is 50.
Where is 54 ÷ 6?

Divide
and
Conquer

Incentive Publications, Inc., Nashville, TN

Divide
and
Conquer

Incentive Publications, Inc., Nashville, TN

Divide
and
Conquer

Incentive Publications, Inc., Nashville, TN

Divide
and
Conquer

Incentive Publications, Inc., Nashville, TN

b.

My number is 7.
Where is 39 ÷ 3?

c.

My number is 6.
Where is 100 ÷ 5?

e.

My number is 30.
Where is 49 ÷ 7?

a.

My number is 13.
Where is 48 ÷ 8?

Divide and Conquer

Incentive Publications, Inc., Nashville, TN

Divide and Conquer

Incentive Publications, Inc., Nashville, TN

Divide and Conquer

Incentive Publications, Inc., Nashville, TN

Divide and Conquer

Incentive Publications, Inc., Nashville, TN

d.

My number is 20.
Where is 200 ÷ 5?

f.

My number is 40.
Where is 99 ÷ 3?

h.

My number is 33.
Where is 180 ÷ 10?

j.

My number is 18.
Where is 50 ÷ 5?

Divide
and
Conquer

Incentive Publications, Inc., Nashville, TN

Divide
and
Conquer

Incentive Publications, Inc., Nashville, TN

Divide
and
Conquer

Incentive Publications, Inc., Nashville, TN

Divide
and
Conquer

Incentive Publications, Inc., Nashville, TN

My number is 11.
Where is 26 ÷ 13?

n.

My number is 22.
Where is 51 ÷ 3?

r.

My number is 10.
Where is 44 ÷ 4?

My number is 2.
Where is 88 ÷ 4?

p.

Incentive Publications, Inc., Nashville, TN

Divide
and
Conquer

Math Connections Game # 6

Incentive Publications, Inc., Nashville, TN

Divide
and
Conquer

Math Connections Game # 6

Incentive Publications, Inc., Nashville, TN

Divide
and
Conquer

Math Connections Game # 6

Incentive Publications, Inc., Nashville, TN

Divide
and
Conquer

Math Connections Game # 6

t.

My number is 17.

Where is 36 ÷ 3?

v.

My number is 12.

Where is 63 ÷ 3?

x.

My number is 21.

Where is 32 ÷ 2?

z.

My number is 16.

Where is 180 ÷ 3?

Divide
and
Conquer

Incentive Publications, Inc., Nashville, TN

Divide
and
Conquer

Incentive Publications, Inc., Nashville, TN

Divide
and
Conquer

Incentive Publications, Inc., Nashville, TN

Divide
and
Conquer

Incentive Publications, Inc., Nashville, TN

bb.

My number is 60.
Where is 30 ÷ 10?

dd.

My number is 3.
Where is 70 ÷ 2?

Math Connections
Game #6

Divide
and
Conquer

A Game to Practice Mental Math Computations
and Reinforce Active Listening

Divide and Conquer

Incentive Publications, Inc., Nashville, TN

Divide and Conquer

Incentive Publications, Inc., Nashville, TN

Math Connections Game # 6

Name _____

SIMPLY DIVIDE

Solve the following problems.

1. $625 \div 25 =$ _____

2. $81 \div 9 =$ _____

3. $144 \div 12 =$ _____

4. $3,800 \div 40 =$ _____

5. $1,250 \div 50 =$ _____

6. $361 \div 19 =$ _____

7. $121 \div 11 =$ _____

8. $100 \div 10 =$ _____

9. $225 \div 15 =$ _____

10. $64 \div 8 =$ _____

11. $25 \div 5 =$ _____

12. $256 \div 16 =$ _____

13. $196 \div 14 =$ _____

14. $169 \div 13 =$ _____

15. $465 \div 5 =$ _____

16. $2,342 \div 2 =$ _____

17. $418 \div 19 =$ _____

18. $390 \div 26 =$ _____

19. $184 : 23 =$ _____

20. $238 \div 14 =$ _____

21. $342 \div 18 =$ _____

22. $208 \div 13 =$ _____

23. $192 \div 12 =$ _____

24. $480 \div 24 =$ _____

©2006 Incentive Publications, Inc., Nashville, TN

Math Connections Game #6

MAKE THE CONNECTIONS

Solve.

1. $150 \div 15 =$ _____

2. $130 \div 10 =$ _____

3. $50 \div 5 =$ _____

4. $2,300 \div 23 =$ _____

5. $470 \div 10 =$ _____

6. $720 \div 72 =$ _____

7. $10,000 \div 100 =$ _____

8. $53,000 \div 53 =$ _____

9. $2,700 \div 27 =$ _____

Solve the following problems.

10. The local store donated bags of outdated candy to the school. They gave 108 bags of candy. The secretary wanted to divide the candy up for each teacher. There were twelve teachers in the school. How many bags of candy will each teacher receive?

_____

11. Mr. Riley had 135 acres of land. He wanted to keep 20 acres for himself and divide the rest among his children. He had three girls and two boys. How many acres of land will each child get from Mr. Riley?

_____

Match.

12. $112 \div 8$ _____   A. 28

13. $126 \div 18$ _____   B. 16

14. $510 \div 34$ _____   C. 14

15. $234 \div 13$ _____   D. 46

16. $546 \div 26$ _____   E. 18

17. $552 \div 12$ _____   F. 7

18. $476 \div 17$ _____   G. 21

19. $384 \div 24$ _____   H. 15

©2006 Incentive Publications, Inc., Nashville, TN

Math Connections Game #6

Here's One for You!

How to Make the Game:

1. Remove pages 121–140 from Math Connections Games.

2. Cut on the lines to make the 30 game cards and the envelope label.

3. Laminate the cards.

4. Glue the label to an envelope or place it inside a plastic portfolio.

5. Place game cards and the Answer Key (page 122) in the envelope. Store the originals for the reproducible pages (pages 139 and 140) in the envelope as well.

Directions:

1. Tell students they will be receiving a card which they should be ready to read aloud.

2. Pass out the cards randomly. Since there are 30 cards, some students may have more than one card.

3. Give students a few minutes to read over their cards.

4. On your signal, one student stands and reads his/her card.

5. Students solve the problems as they are read, and read their cards at the appropriate times. The game proceeds until every student has participated. The very last problem read in the game should have been answered by the number read to begin the game.

Two reproducible activity pages are included with each Math Connections game. Use these pages to introduce the math skills before playing the game and to reinforce the skills after playing the game.

The answer is 1 bar.

Here's one for you.
If Josie has six sets of eight jelly bracelets, how many bracelets does she have in all?

aa.
The answer is 48 bracelets.

Here's one for you.
Each puppy gets four doggie chews after training. If there are seven dogs in the class, how many doggie chews does the instructor need?

y.
The answer is 28 chews.

Here's one for you.
On the field trip, the five group members each collected nine fossils. How many fossils did the group find in all?

w.
The answer is 45 fossils.

Here's one for you.
The photographer took seven pictures of seven different flowers. How many photos did she take in all?

Math Connections
Game #7

Here's One
for You!

A Game to Improve Listening Skills
as Students Solve Word Problems
with Mental Math

page 139

page 140

©2006 INCENTIVE PUBLICATIONS, Inc., Nashville, TN

HERE'S ONE FOR YOU!

Monitor student responses and prompt students, as necessary, through the game. You may choose a student monitor to be the prompter. This key represents the responses in one possible order.

In this game, any card may begin. Have the monitor choose the person to begin and find that person's card on the key using the small letter(s) on the upper left-hand corner of the card. The beginning reader should read only the black part (the problem) on his or her card. The correct order will move down from that card, back up to the top, and then down to the starting card. If played correctly, all students will have read their card aloud, and the answer to the last problem will be on the card of the person beginning the game.

cc. The answer is 1 bar. Here's one for you. If Josie has six sets of eight jelly bracelets, how many bracelets does she have in all?

aa. The answer is 48 bracelets. Here's one for you. Each puppy gets four doggie chews after training. If there are seven dogs in the class, how many doggie chews does the instructor need?

y. The answer is 28 chews. Here's one for you. On the field trip, the five group members each collected nine fossils. How many fossils did the group find in all?

w. The answer is 45 fossils. Here's one for you. The photographer took seven pictures of seven different flowers. How many photos did she take in all?

u. The answer is 49 photos. Here's one for you. There are three sets of eight steps that lead to the tree house. How many steps are there is all?

s. The answer is 24 steps. Here's one for you. The office manager bought 36 pens. He put an equal number of pens at each station. There are 6 stations. How many did he put at each station?

q. The answer is 6 pens. Here's one for you. We need 90 chairs in the auditorium. Mr. Ruiz wants nine chairs in each row. How many rows will there be?

o. The answer is 10 rows. Here's one for you. The class is dividing the textbooks into four equal stacks. There are 44 textbooks in all. How many will be in each stack?

m. The answer is 11 textbooks. Here's one for you. Mrs. Layden bought nine 8-packs of batteries. How many batteries did she buy in all?

k. The answer is 72 batteries. Here's one for you. The junior varsity and the varsity cheerleading teams each have seven members. How many cheerleaders are there in all?

i. The answer is 14 cheerleaders. Here's one for you. The sandwiches for the picnic arrived in 45 coolers. If the picnic organizers can put five coolers on a table, how many tables will they need to set up?

g. The answer is 9 tables. Here's one for you. Eight choir members each organized seven music portfolios. How many portfolios are organized?

e. The answer is 56 portfolios. Here's one for you. Six parents volunteer eight hours a month in the library. How many hours do the volunteers work?

b. The answer is 48 hours. Here's one for you. The coach organized 63 jump ropes on nine hooks. If she put the same number on each hook, how many was that?

a. The answer is 7 jump ropes. Here's one for you. Four vans carried eight students to the math competition. How many students went to the competition?

c. The answer is 32 students. Here's one for you. The six biology classes each dissected three pig eyes. How many pig eyes were dissected in all?

d. The answer is 18 eyes. Here's one for you. The office gave out 33 visitor passes in one day. If the same number of visitors went to each of the 11 classrooms, how many visitors were there in each room?

f. The answer is 3 visitors. Here's one for you. There are 24 students in gym class. If the coach wants teams of 12, how many teams can he form?

h. The answer is 2 teams. Here's one for you. The art class has seven tables with five students at each table. How many students are taking art?

j. The answer is 35 students. Here's one for you. Anna is planning to make a quilt with nine rows of four quilt blocks per row. How many quilt blocks will she need in all?

l. The answer is 36 quilt blocks. Here's one for you. Jose has organized his collection of model cars onto seven shelves. If he has 35 cars in all and puts the same number on each shelf, how many cars are on a shelf?

n. The answer is 5 cars. Here's one for you. The lunchroom has 64 tables. If the tables are organized in eight equal rows, how many tables are in each row?

p. The answer is 8 tables. Here's one for you. Eleven students paid $5.00 each to get the new study guide. How much did they pay in all?

r. The answer is $55.00. Here's one for you. Mr. Rupp will divide the writing class into response groups of three persons each. If there are 36 students in class, how many groups will there be?

t. The answer is 12 groups. Here's one for you. On the west side of the building, seven classrooms have seven windows each. How many windows are on the west side of the building?

v. The answer is 49 windows. Here's one for you. Three parents have volunteered to chaperone Ms. Lee's class of 45 students on the field trip. If each parent has the same sized group, how many students will be in each group?

x. The answer is 15 students. Here's one for you. Nine mothers each brought three cakes for the cakewalk. How many cakes are there in all?

z. The answer is 27 cakes. Here's one for you. The school must add 48 new lockers. If twelve lockers can be put in a hallway, how many hallways will have new lockers?

bb. The answer is 4 hallways. Here's one for you. Five students must memorize five different pages of facts for the knowledge bowl. How many pages of facts will they memorize?

dd. The answer is 25 pages. Here's one for you. The lunch lady had 29 trays and 29 snack bars. How many bars can she put on each tray?

122

©2006 INCENTIVE PUBLICATIONS, Inc., Nashville, TN

aa.

The answer is 48 bracelets.

Here's one for you.
Each puppy gets four doggie chews after training. If there are seven dogs in the class, how many doggie chews does the instructor need?

The answer is 1 bar.

Here's one for you.
If Josie has six sets of eight jelly bracelets, how many bracelets does she have in all?

---

w.

The answer is 45 fossils.

Here's one for you.
The photographer took seven pictures of seven different flowers. How many photos did she take in all?

---

y.

The answer is 28 chews.

Here's one for you.
On the field trip, the five group members each collected nine fossils. How many fossils did the group find in all?

Here's One
for You

Incentive Publications, Inc., Nashville, TN

Here's One
for You

Incentive Publications, Inc., Nashville, TN

Here's One
for You

Incentive Publications, Inc., Nashville, TN

Here's One
for You

Incentive Publications, Inc., Nashville, TN

u.

The answer is 49 photos.

Here's one for you.
There are three sets of eight steps that lead to the tree house. How many steps are there is all?

q.

The answer is 6 pens.

Here's one for you.
We need 90 chairs in the auditorium. Mr. Ruiz wants nine chairs in each row. How many rows will there be?

s.

The answer is 24 steps.

Here's one for you.
The office manager bought 36 pens. He put an equal number of pens at each station. There are 6 stations. How many did he put at each station?

o.

The answer is 10 rows.

Here's one for you.
The class is dividing the textbooks into four equal stacks. There are 44 textbooks in all. How many will be in each stack?

Incentive Publications, Inc., Nashville, TN

Here's One for You

Incentive Publications, Inc., Nashville, TN

Here's One for You

Incentive Publications, Inc., Nashville, TN

Here's One for You

Incentive Publications, Inc., Nashville, TN

Here's One for You

m.

The answer is 11 textbooks.

Here's one for you.
Mrs. Layden bought nine 8-packs of batteries. How many batteries did she buy in all?

k.

The answer is 72 batteries.

Here's one for you.
The junior varsity and the varsity cheerleading teams each have seven members. How many cheerleaders are there in all?

i.

The answer is 14 cheerleaders.

Here's one for you.
The sandwiches for the picnic arrived in 45 coolers. If the picnic organizers can put five coolers on a table, how many tables will they need to set up?

g.

The answer is 9 tables.

Here's one for you.
Eight choir members each organized seven music portfolios. How many portfolios are organized?

Incentive Publications, Inc., Nashville, TN

Here's One for You

Incentive Publications, Inc., Nashville, TN

Here's One for You

Incentive Publications, Inc., Nashville, TN

Here's One for You

Incentive Publications, Inc., Nashville, TN

Here's One for You

e.

The answer is 56 portfolios.

Here's one for you.
Six parents volunteer eight hours a month in the library. How many hours do the volunteers work?

a.

The answer is 7 jump ropes.

Here's one for you.
Four vans carried eight students to the math competition. How many students went to the competition?

b.

The answer is 54 hours.

Here's one for you.
The coach organized 63 jump ropes on nine hooks. If she put the same number on each hook, how many was that?

c.

The answer is 32 students.

Here's one for you.
The six biology classes each dissected three pig eyes. How many pig eyes were dissected in all?

Incentive Publications, Inc., Nashville, TN

Here's One for You

Incentive Publications, Inc., Nashville, TN

Here's One for You

Incentive Publications, Inc., Nashville, TN

Here's One for You

Incentive Publications, Inc., Nashville, TN

Here's One for You

d.

The answer is 18 eyes.

Here's one for you.
The office gave out 33 visitor passes in one day. If the same number of visitors went to each of the 11 classrooms, how many visitors were there in each room?

f.

The answer is 3 visitors.

Here's one for you.
There are 24 students in gym class. If the coach wants teams of 12, how many teams can he form?

h.

The answer is 2 teams.

Here's one for you.
The art class has seven tables with five students at each table. How many students are taking art?

j.

The answer is 35 students.

Here's one for you.
Anna is planning to make a quilt with nine rows of four quilt blocks per row. How many quilt blocks will she need in all?

Incentive Publications, Inc., Nashville, TN

Here's One
for You

Math Connections Game # 7

Incentive Publications, Inc., Nashville, TN

Here's One
for You

Math Connections Game # 7

Incentive Publications, Inc., Nashville, TN

Here's One
for You

Math Connections Game # 7

Incentive Publications, Inc., Nashville, TN

Here's One
for You

Math Connections Game # 7

l.

The answer is 36 quilt blocks.

Here's one for you.
Jose has organized his collection of model cars onto seven shelves. If he has 35 cars in all and puts the same number on each shelf, how many cars are on a shelf?

n.

The answer is 5 cars.

Here's one for you.
The lunchroom has 64 tables. If the tables are organized in eight equal rows, how many tables are in each row?

p.

The answer is 8 tables.

Here's one for you.
Eleven students paid $5.00 each to get the new study guide. How much did they pay in all?

r.

The answer is $55.00.

Here's one for you.
Mr. Rupp will divide the writing class into response groups of three persons each. If there are 36 students in class, how many groups will there be?

Here's One
for You

Incentive Publications, Inc., Nashville, TN

Math Connections Game # 7

Here's One
for You

Incentive Publications, Inc., Nashville, TN

Math Connections Game # 7

Here's One
for You

Incentive Publications, Inc., Nashville, TN

Math Connections Game # 7

Here's One
for You

Incentive Publications, Inc., Nashville, TN

Math Connections Game # 7

t.

The answer is 12 groups.

Here's one for you.
On the west side of the building, seven classrooms have seven windows each. How many windows are on the west side of the building?

v.

The answer is 49 windows.

Here's one for you.
Three parents have volunteered to chaperone Ms. Lee's class of 45 students on the field trip. If each parent has the same-sized group, how many students will be in each group?

x.

The answer is 15 students.

Here's one for you.
Nine mothers each brought three cakes for the cakewalk. How many cakes are there in all?

z.

The answer is 27 cakes.

Here's one for you.
The school must add 48 new lockers. If twelve lockers can be put in a hallway, how many hallways will have new lockers?

Incentive Publications, Inc., Nashville, TN

Here's One
for You

Incentive Publications, Inc., Nashville, TN

Here's One
for You

Incentive Publications, Inc., Nashville, TN

Here's One
for You

Incentive Publications, Inc., Nashville, TN

Here's One
for You

bb.

The answer is 4 hallways.

Here's one for you.
Five students must memorize five different pages of facts for the knowledge bowl. How many pages of facts will they memorize?

dd.

The answer is 25 pages.

Here's one for you.
The lunch lady had 29 trays and 29 snack bars. How many bars can she put on each tray?

Math Connections
Game #7

Here's One for You!

A Game to Improve Listening Skills as Students Solve Word Problems with Mental Math

Incentive Publications, Inc., Nashville, TN

Here's One for You

Incentive Publications, Inc., Nashville, TN

Here's One for You

THAT'S A FACT!

Carefully read these statements about multiplication and division. Mark each statement true or false. If the statement is false, correct it to make it true.

_____ 1. Multiplication could be called repeated fractions.

_____ 2. Any number multiplied by zero is zero.

_____ 3. In a multiplication problem, the numbers that are being multiplied are called factors.

_____ 4. The answer to a multiplication problem is the sum.

_____ 5. Any number multiplied by one is one.

_____ 6. Division could be called repeated subtraction.

_____ 7. Division is a way of finding out how many times one number (the divisor) will fit into another number (the dividend).

_____ 8. The answer in division is called the difference.

_____ 9. If a divisor does not go into the dividend an even number of times, there is a number left over. The number is called the result.

_____ 10. A number is divisible by another number if the quotient of the two numbers is a mixed number.

_____ 11. A number is divisible by 5 only if the last digit is 0 or 5.

_____ 12. A number is divisible by 2 only if the last digit is 2.

_____ 13. Multiplication and addition are inverse operations.

_____ 14. The Identity Property of Multiplication says that the product of 1 and any number is that number.

_____ 15. The Distributive Property of Multiplication requires that when you are multiplying a sum of numbers, you add the numbers in parentheses before multiplying them.

©2006 Incentive Publications, Inc., Nashville, TN

Math Connections Game #7

Name _____

SPORTS MEMORABILIA

Sarah's aunt and uncle are great sports fans. They love to watch their favorite athletes and teams on TV or at live sporting events. But they also enjoy collecting memorabilia that was used by famous sports personalities or collectibles that commemorate their famous accomplishments.

1. Sarah's aunt has an interest in the Triple Crown of Racing: the Kentucky Derby, the Preakness Stakes, and the Belmont Stakes. She collects the official race day glasses from the three races and she also collects figurines of the horses that have won the races. Sarah has decided to total the value of her aunt's collection.

Number in Collection	Description of Item	Value of One	Total Value
5	1995 Kentucky Derby glass	$2	_____
3	1994 Triple Crown glasses (set)	$9	_____
7	1989 Belmont Stakes cup	$4	_____
4	Triple Crown horses (set)	$23	_____
8	Secretariat figurines	$6	_____
		Total Value of Collection	_____

2. Sarah's uncle is a baseball fan, and his blood runs "Cincinnati Red." He collects rookie cards, signed baseballs, programs, and felt pennants.

Number in Collection	Description of Item	Value of One	Total Value
9	Baseballs signed by Opening Day starters	$12	_____
6	Complete Rookie Card Sets (1995)	$29	_____
7	2000 World Series Programs	$8	_____
27	Felt Pennants (assorted teams)	$4	_____
3	Baseballs signed by Hal Morris	$7	_____
		Total Value	_____

3. Both Sarah's aunt and uncle are golf fans. Their favorite tournament is the Masters at Augusta. Their favorite golfer is Tiger Woods.

Number in Collection	Description of Item	Value of One	Total Value
5	Programs from the Masters	$7	_____
3	1996 passes signed by Greg Norman	$14	_____
7	Golf balls used by Lee Trevino	$6	_____
2	Golf hats worn by Tiger Woods	$58	_____
9	Gold tees used by Tiger Woods	$2	_____
		Total Value	_____

©2006 Incentive Publications, Inc., Nashville, TN

Math Connections Game #7

Just a Fraction

How to Make the Game:

1. Remove pages 141–160 from Math Connections Games.

2. Cut on the lines to make the 30 game cards and the envelope label.

3. Laminate the cards.

4. Glue the label to an envelope or place it inside a plastic portfolio.

5. Place game cards and Answer Key (page 142) in the envelope. Store the originals for the reproducible pages (pages 159 and 160) in the envelope as well.

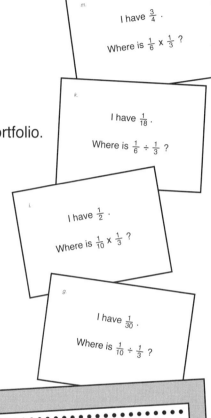

Directions:

1. Tell students they will be receiving a card which they should be ready to read aloud.

2. Pass out the cards randomly. Since there are 30 cards, some students may have more than one card.

3. Give students a few minutes to read over their cards.

4. On your signal, one student stands and reads his/her card.

5. Students solve the problems as they are read, and read their cards at the appropriate times. The game proceeds until every student has participated. The very last problem read in the game should have been answered by the number read to begin the game.

Two reproducible activity pages are included with each Math Connections game. Use these pages to introduce the math skills before playing the game and to reinforce the skills after playing the game.

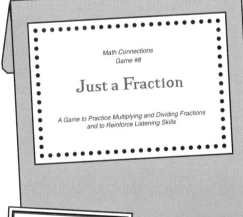

page 159

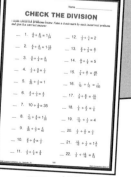

page 160

JUST A FRACTION

Monitor student responses and prompt students, as necessary, through the game. You may choose a student monitor to be the prompter. This key represents the responses in one possible order. In this game, any card may begin. Have the monitor choose the person to begin and find that person's card on the key using the small letter(s) on the upper left-hand corner of the card. The beginning reader should read only the black part (the question) on his or her card. The correct order will move down from that card, back up to the top, and then down to the starting card. If played correctly, all students will have read their card aloud, and the last problem will be answered correctly by the "I have . . ." statement on the card of the person who started the game.

cc. I have $\frac{5}{8}$. Where is $\frac{1}{2} \times \frac{1}{4}$?

c. I have $\frac{1}{24}$. Where is $\frac{1}{6} \div \frac{1}{4}$?

aa. I have $\frac{1}{8}$. Where is $\frac{1}{2} \div \frac{1}{4}$?

d. I have $\frac{2}{3}$. Where is $\frac{1}{8} \times \frac{1}{2}$?

y. I have 2. Where is $\frac{1}{3} \times \frac{1}{3}$?

f. I have $\frac{1}{16}$. Where is $\frac{1}{8} \div \frac{1}{2}$?

w. I have $\frac{1}{9}$. Where is $\frac{1}{3} \div \frac{1}{3}$?

h. I have $\frac{1}{4}$. Where is $\frac{1}{3} \times \frac{1}{7}$?

u. I have 1. Where is $\frac{1}{2} \times \frac{1}{5}$?

j. I have $\frac{1}{21}$. Where is $\frac{1}{3} \div \frac{1}{7}$?

s. I have $\frac{1}{10}$. Where is $\frac{1}{5} \div \frac{1}{2}$?

l. I have $2\frac{1}{3}$. Where is $\frac{1}{6} \times \frac{1}{9}$?

q. I have $\frac{2}{5}$. Where is $\frac{1}{4} \times \frac{1}{3}$?

n. I have $\frac{1}{54}$. Where is $\frac{1}{6} \div \frac{1}{9}$?

o. I have $\frac{1}{12}$. Where is $\frac{1}{4} \div \frac{1}{3}$?

p. I have $1\frac{1}{2}$. Where is $\frac{1}{7} \times \frac{1}{4}$?

m. I have $\frac{3}{4}$. Where is $\frac{1}{6} \times \frac{1}{3}$?

r. I have $\frac{1}{28}$. Where is $\frac{1}{4} \div \frac{1}{7}$?

k. I have $\frac{1}{18}$. Where is $\frac{1}{6} \div \frac{1}{3}$?

t. I have $1\frac{3}{4}$. Where is $\frac{1}{8} \times \frac{1}{4}$?

i. I have $\frac{1}{2}$. Where is $\frac{1}{10} \times \frac{1}{3}$?

v. I have $\frac{1}{32}$. Where is $\frac{1}{8} \div \frac{1}{3}$?

g. I have $\frac{1}{30}$. Where is $\frac{1}{10} \div \frac{1}{3}$?

x. I have $\frac{3}{8}$. Where is $\frac{1}{9} \times \frac{1}{3}$?

e. I have $\frac{3}{10}$. Where is $\frac{1}{5} \times \frac{1}{4}$?

z. I have $\frac{1}{27}$. Where is $\frac{1}{9} \div \frac{1}{3}$?

b. I have $\frac{1}{20}$. Where is $\frac{1}{4} \div \frac{1}{5}$?

bb. I have $\frac{1}{3}$. Where is $\frac{1}{8} \times \frac{1}{5}$?

a. I have $1\frac{1}{4}$. Where is $\frac{1}{4} \times \frac{1}{6}$?

dd. I have $\frac{1}{40}$. Where is $\frac{1}{8} \div \frac{1}{5}$?

©2006 Incentive Publications, Inc., Nashville, TN

aa.

I have $\frac{1}{8}$.

Where is $\frac{1}{2} \div \frac{1}{4}$?

---

w.

I have $\frac{1}{9}$.

Where is $\frac{1}{3} \div \frac{1}{3}$?

---

cc.

I have $\frac{5}{8}$.

Where is $\frac{1}{2} \times \frac{1}{4}$?

---

y.

I have 2.

Where is $\frac{1}{3} \times \frac{1}{3}$?

Incentive Publications, Inc., Nashville, TN

Just
a
Fraction

Math Connections Game # 8

Incentive Publications, Inc., Nashville, TN

Just
a
Fraction

Math Connections Game # 8

Incentive Publications, Inc., Nashville, TN

Just
a
Fraction

Math Connections Game # 8

Incentive Publications, Inc., Nashville, TN

Just
a
Fraction

Math Connections Game # 8

s.

I have $\frac{1}{10}$.

Where is $\frac{1}{5} \div \frac{1}{2}$?

o.

I have $\frac{1}{12}$.

Where is $\frac{1}{4} \div \frac{1}{3}$?

u.

I have 1 .

Where is $\frac{1}{2} \times \frac{1}{5}$?

q.

I have $\frac{2}{5}$.

Where is $\frac{1}{4} \times \frac{1}{3}$?

Incentive Publications, Inc., Nashville, TN

Just
a
Fraction

Incentive Publications, Inc., Nashville, TN

Just
a
Fraction

Incentive Publications, Inc., Nashville, TN

Just
a
Fraction

Incentive Publications, Inc., Nashville, TN

Just
a
Fraction

m.

I have $\frac{3}{4}$.

Where is $\frac{1}{6} \times \frac{1}{3}$?

k.

I have $\frac{1}{18}$.

Where is $\frac{1}{6} \div \frac{1}{3}$?

i.

I have $\frac{1}{2}$.

Where is $\frac{1}{10} \times \frac{1}{3}$?

g.

I have $\frac{1}{30}$.

Where is $\frac{1}{10} \div \frac{1}{3}$?

Incentive Publications, Inc., Nashville, TN

Just
a
Fraction

Incentive Publications, Inc., Nashville, TN

Just
a
Fraction

Incentive Publications, Inc., Nashville, TN

Just
a
Fraction

Incentive Publications, Inc., Nashville, TN

Just
a
Fraction

b.

I have $\frac{1}{20}$.

Where is $\frac{1}{4} \div \frac{1}{5}$?

c.

I have $\frac{1}{24}$.

Where is $\frac{1}{6} \div \frac{1}{4}$?

e.

I have $\frac{3}{10}$.

Where is $\frac{1}{5} \times \frac{1}{4}$?

a.

I have $1\frac{1}{4}$.

Where is $\frac{1}{4} \times \frac{1}{6}$?

Just
a
Fraction

Incentive Publications, Inc., Nashville, TN

Math Connections Game # 8

Just
a
Fraction

Incentive Publications, Inc., Nashville, TN

Math Connections Game # 8

Just
a
Fraction

Incentive Publications, Inc., Nashville, TN

Math Connections Game # 8

Just
a
Fraction

Incentive Publications, Inc., Nashville, TN

Math Connections Game # 8

d.

I have $\frac{2}{3}$.

Where is $\frac{1}{8} \times \frac{1}{2}$?

f.

I have $\frac{1}{16}$.

Where is $\frac{1}{8} \div \frac{1}{2}$?

h.

I have $\frac{1}{4}$.

Where is $\frac{1}{3} \times \frac{1}{7}$?

j.

I have $\frac{1}{21}$.

Where is $\frac{1}{3} \div \frac{1}{7}$?

Just
a
Fraction

Incentive Publications, Inc., Nashville, TN

Just
a
Fraction

Incentive Publications, Inc., Nashville, TN

Just
a
Fraction

Incentive Publications, Inc., Nashville, TN

Just
a
Fraction

Incentive Publications, Inc., Nashville, TN

n.

I have $\frac{1}{54}$.

Where is $\frac{1}{6} \div \frac{1}{9}$?

---

l.

I have $2\frac{1}{3}$.

Where is $\frac{1}{6} \times \frac{1}{9}$?

---

r.

I have $\frac{1}{28}$.

Where is $\frac{1}{4} \div \frac{1}{7}$?

---

p.

I have $1\frac{1}{2}$.

Where is $\frac{1}{7} \times \frac{1}{4}$?

Incentive Publications, Inc., Nashville, TN

Just
a
Fraction

Math Connections Game # 8

Incentive Publications, Inc., Nashville, TN

Just
a
Fraction

Math Connections Game # 8

Incentive Publications, Inc., Nashville, TN

Just
a
Fraction

Math Connections Game # 8

Incentive Publications, Inc., Nashville, TN

Just
a
Fraction

Math Connections Game # 8

t.

I have $1\frac{3}{4}$.

Where is $\frac{1}{8} \times \frac{1}{4}$?

v.

I have $\frac{1}{32}$.

Where is $\frac{1}{8} \div \frac{1}{3}$?

x.

I have $\frac{3}{8}$.

Where is $\frac{1}{9} \times \frac{1}{3}$?

z.

I have $\frac{1}{27}$.

Where is $\frac{1}{9} \div \frac{1}{3}$?

Incentive Publications, Inc., Nashville, TN

Just
a
Fraction

Incentive Publications, Inc., Nashville, TN

Just
a
Fraction

Incentive Publications, Inc., Nashville, TN

Just
a
Fraction

Incentive Publications, Inc., Nashville, TN

Just
a
Fraction

bb.

I have $\frac{1}{3}$.

Where is $\frac{1}{8} \times \frac{1}{5}$?

dd.

I have $\frac{1}{40}$.

Where is $\frac{1}{8} \div \frac{1}{5}$?

Math Connections
Game #8

Just a Fraction

A Game to Practice Multiplying and Dividing Fractions
and to Reinforce Listening Skills

Incentive Publications, Inc., Nashville, TN

Just
a
Fraction

Incentive Publications, Inc., Nashville, TN

Just
a
Fraction

HOW MUCH DO YOU NEED?

1. The caterers for the awards assembly need to calculate how much food to serve the guests. There will be 160 guests at the reception. Calculate the amount for the caterers to order.

Food Item	Amount/Person	Total Amount to Order
mints	$\frac{1}{32}$ pound	a. _____
pizza	$\frac{1}{8}$ pie	b. _____
nuts	$\frac{3}{40}$ pound	c. _____
punch	$\frac{5}{32}$ gallon	d. _____
cookies	$\frac{1}{16}$ pound	e. _____
fudge	$\frac{3}{64}$ pound	f. _____

2. The caterers are also preparing a picnic for the student council following the assembly. There will be 48 council members attending.

Food Item	Amount/Person	Total Amount to Order
hot-dogs	$\frac{1}{10}$ pound	g. _____
hot-dog buns	$\frac{1}{12}$ dozen	h. _____
mustard	$\frac{1}{4}$ ounce	i. _____
ketchup	$\frac{1}{3}$ ounce	j. _____
hamburger	$\frac{1}{5}$ pound	k. _____
hamburger bun	$\frac{1}{12}$ dozen	l. _____
potato chips	$\frac{3}{16}$ pound	m. _____
baked beans	$\frac{3}{8}$ cup	n. _____
jello	$\frac{1}{24}$ pan	o. _____
ice cream	$\frac{3}{32}$ pound	p. _____

©2006 Incentive Publications, Inc., Nashville, TN

Math Connections Game #8

CHECK THE DIVISION

Please check the problems below. Make a check mark by each incorrect problem and give the correct answer.

___ 1. $\frac{5}{6} \div \frac{8}{15} = 1\frac{1}{24}$

___ 2. $\frac{4}{9} \div \frac{3}{10} = 1\frac{13}{27}$

___ 3. $\frac{5}{8} \div \frac{1}{2} = \frac{5}{16}$

___ 4. $\frac{1}{2} \div \frac{5}{8} = \frac{1}{2}$

___ 5. $\frac{5}{25} \div \frac{1}{5} = 1$

___ 6. $\frac{4}{3} \div \frac{1}{3} = \frac{4}{3}$

___ 7. $10 \div \frac{3}{8} = 35$

___ 8. $\frac{7}{10} \div \frac{4}{6} = 1\frac{1}{20}$

___ 9. $\frac{9}{20} \div \frac{1}{3} = \frac{3}{40}$

___ 10. $\frac{2}{5} \div \frac{4}{5} = \frac{1}{2}$

___ 11. $\frac{1}{3} \div \frac{1}{3} = \frac{3}{9}$

___ 12. $\frac{1}{2} \div \frac{1}{4} = 2$

___ 13. $\frac{2}{3} \div \frac{7}{9} = \frac{6}{7}$

___ 14. $\frac{5}{9} \div \frac{1}{9} = 5$

___ 15. $\frac{7}{9} \div \frac{9}{7} = \frac{49}{81}$

___ 16. $\frac{1}{10} \div \frac{1}{10} = \frac{1}{100}$

___ 17. $\frac{7}{8} \div \frac{6}{9} = \frac{15}{16}$

___ 18. $\frac{1}{2} \div \frac{2}{3} = \frac{1}{6}$

___ 19. $\frac{11}{12} \div \frac{1}{2} = 4$

___ 20. $\frac{1}{3} \div \frac{2}{3} = \frac{1}{2}$

___ 21. $\frac{12}{15} \div \frac{1}{2} = 1\frac{3}{5}$

___ 22. $\frac{1}{3} \div \frac{13}{18} = \frac{6}{13}$

©2006 INCENTIVE PUBLICATIONS, Inc., Nashville, TN

Math Connections Game #?